Buddhism

Sue Penney

Heinemann
LIBRARY

www.heinemann.co.uk
Visit our website to find out more information about Heinemann Library books.

To order:
☎ Phone 44 (0) 1865 888066
🖹 Send a fax to 44 (0) 1865 314091
💻 Visit the Heinemann Bookshop at www.heinemann.co.uk to browse our catalogue and order online.

First published in Great Britain by Heinemann Library
Halley Court, Jordan Hill, Oxford OX2 8EJ
a division of Reed Educational and Professional Publishing Ltd.
Heinemann is a registered trademark of Reed Educational & Professional Publishing Ltd.

OXFORD   MELBOURNE   AUCKLAND
JOHANNESBURG   BLANTYRE   GABORONE
IBADAN   PORTSMOUTH (NH) USA   CHICAGO

Designed by Ken Vail Graphic Design, Cambridge
Originated by Universal
Printed in Hong Kong by Wing King Tong.

ISBN 0 431 09311 3 (hardback)   ISBN 0 431 09318 0 (paperback)
04 03 02 01   05 04 03 02 01
10 9 8 7 6 5 4 3 2   10 9 8 7 6 5 4 3 2

This book is also available in hardback (ISBN 0 431 09311 3).

British Library Cataloguing in Publication Data
Penney, Sue
Buddhism. – (World Beliefs and Cultures)
1. Buddhism
1. Title
294.3

Acknowledgements
The publishers would like to thank the following for permission to reproduce copyright material: All quotations are from *The Dhammapada*, Pengin Books, 1973 © Renguin Books Ltd 1973. Reproduced by permission of Penguin Books Ltd.

The Publishers would like to thank the following for permission to reproduce photographs: Andes Press Agency p. 38; Ann & Bury Peerless, pp. 13, 34; Associated Press p. 27; Carlos Reyes-Manzo, Andes Press Agency p.5; Circa Photo Library pp. 11, 15, 20, /William Holtby pp. 22, 25, 32, 39, /John Smith p. 23; Corbis p. 29; Hutchison Library, pp. 4, 7, 8, 10, 12, 18, 19, 24, 40, 42, /Carlos Freire p. 28, /Michael Macintyre pp. 30, 33; Impact pp.14, 37, /Mark Henley p. 26, /Dominic Sansoni p. 35; Phil & Val Emmett p. 6; Robin Bath pp. 17, 21, 31, 36, 41, 43.

Cover photograph reproduced with permission of E. T. Archive

Our thanks to Philip Emmett for his comments in the preparation of this book.

Every effort has been made to contact copyright holders of any material reproduced in this book. Any omissions will be rectified in subsequent printings if notice is given to the Publisher.

Words appearing in the text in bold, **like this**, are explained in the Glossary.

Contents

Dates: In this book, dates are followed by the letters BCE (Before the Common Era) or CE (Common Era). This is instead of using BC (Before Christ) and AD (*Anno Domini* meaning in the year of our Lord). The date numbers are the same in both systems.

Introducing Buddhism

The teachings we call Buddhism began in India about 2500 years ago. The teacher was a man called Siddattha Gotama, whom his followers call the Buddha. Buddha is a special title which means someone who has gained **Enlightenment**. Enlightenment is a special understanding – realizing the truth about the way things are. Buddhists believe that there were other Buddhas before Siddattha, and there will be others in the future, but he is the one whose teachings are for the present age.

What do Buddhists believe?

Buddhists believe that everything in the world is imperfect, and that nothing lasts. They believe that when the Buddha gained Enlightenment, he found the answer to why this is so, and how to overcome it. They believe that if people follow the teachings of the Buddha they, too, can gain Enlightenment. This means that many Buddhists believe everyone could become a Buddha. Buddhists do not believe in an all-powerful God. Their teachings have no need of such a being. They do not believe that the Buddha himself was anything more than a human being. He is important because he achieved Enlightenment and chose to teach others the way to achieve it, too.

Nirvana

Buddists believe in a continual cycle of birth, old age, illness, death and 'rebecoming' or **rebirth**. They do not believe in **reincarnation** (a soul being reborn in a different body), as they do not believe in a soul. This cycle of life is described in the word **samsara**. Buddhists believe that the only escape is to gain Enlightenment. This will allow them to achieve **Nirvana**, which is the end of imperfection. Buddhists say that because everything in this world is imperfect, there are no words which can describe Nirvana. They say that it is the 'blowing out of the fires' of greed, hatred and ignorance, followed by a state of perfect peace.

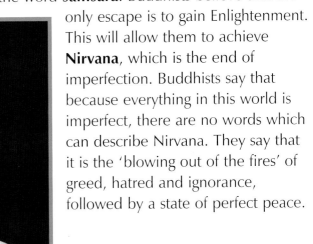

◀ *The lotus flower is used by Buddists as a symbol because it rises out of the mud to become a beautiful flower.*

Meditation

Buddhists try to reach Nirvana by following the Buddha's teachings. These include **meditation**, which is training your mind so that you can empty it of all thoughts, and focus only on things that are really important. They aim to control their minds so that they can go 'beyond' thought. This means that they can leave behind all worries about the world and their life, and rise above them. Buddhists believe that by meditating they will become better people, and will be able to achieve Enlightenment.

Buddhism is not a religion in the strict sense. Many Buddhists prefer to call it a system of thought or **philosophy**. This means they dislike words that are normally used in religions being used about Buddhists – for example, 'worship'. In this book, worship means the way Buddhists practise their beliefs. It does not suggest that Buddhists are looking for God.

▲ *Meditation is an important part of Buddhist worship.*

Buddhism: quick reference

- The teaching we call Buddhism began in India about 500 BCE.

- Buddhists follow the teachings of Siddattha Gotama, called the Buddha.

- Buddhists worship in temples and at home.

- The major teachings of Buddhism are the Tipitaka, which means 'three baskets'.

- The symbol used for Buddhism is a wheel with eight spokes. The wheel is a reminder of the cycle of samsara, the eight spokes are a reminder that one of the Buddha's most important teachings was divided into eight parts. Another symbol is the lotus flower. This grows in mud, but rises to the top of the pond as a beautiful flower. Buddhists say it is a symbol of rising above everything imperfect in this life.

- No one is sure exactly how many Buddhists there are in the world. Some worship at home and do not attend temples. Some live in countries such as Tibet where official statistics are not collected. In 1999, the official figure was around 350 million. Other people suggest figures between 230 and 500 million. There are about 401,000 Buddhists in the US, about 199,000 in Australia and about 135,000 in the UK.

The life of the Buddha

▲ *This tree at Anuradhapura in Sri Lanka grew from a cutting taken from the one at Bodh Gaya. It may be the oldest tree in the world.*

The bodhi tree

The bodhi tree is a sort of fig tree. In 250 BCE, a cutting from the tree at Bodh Gaya was taken to Sri Lanka, when Buddhism was introduced there, and planted. This tree is still alive, and is believed to be the oldest tree in the world. The original tree at Bodh Gaya died in the twelfth century CE, but in 1884 a cutting from the tree in Sri Lanka was taken back there. The tree grew, and Buddhists today can sit under it to meditate.

Siddattha Gotama was an Indian prince. He was born at Lumbini, in what is today called Nepal, in the sixth century BCE.

The stories say that when Siddattha was born, a wise man said that if he ever saw suffering, he would become a great religious leader rather than a great ruler. Siddattha's father wanted an heir to succeed him, so he ordered that no one who was sick or old should be allowed near the prince. Siddattha himself was not allowed to leave the palace grounds. Siddattha grew up to be handsome and clever. He married a beautiful girl, and they had a son. He was rich and powerful – it seemed that his life had everything.

However, Siddattha became bored with his sheltered life and one day he went riding outside the palace grounds. While he was out he saw an old man, a sick man and a funeral, with relatives weeping around the body. These things disturbed him very much. Then he saw a holy man who was contented and happy. He said he had given up his home and his family, and wandered from place to place searching for the answers to the problem of suffering in the world.

Siddattha was so troubled by what he had seen that he decided he, too, must try to find the answer to this problem. On the night before his 29th birthday, he left the palace. He changed his royal robes for the simple clothes worn by holy men, and shaved his head.

Siddattha's search for Enlightenment

For the next six years, Siddattha travelled around India. He spent some time with two great teachers, then with a group of **monks**. For several years he lived with five holy men, eating and drinking almost nothing. But he found that starving himself did not help him to find any answers, so he began eating and drinking again. The holy men left him in disgust, thinking he had given up searching. Siddattha travelled on until at last he came to a great tree. Today this is called the **bodhi tree**, which means 'tree of wisdom', and the place is called Bodh Gaya. He sat under the tree and meditated.

You can find the places mentioned in this book on the map on page 44.

Buddhists believe that during this time, Siddattha was attacked by the evil spirit Mara who sent demons to scare him and tried to tempt him away from his **meditation**. The attack had no effect. At last – the stories say on the night of the full moon, his 35th birthday – Siddattha gained **Enlightenment**. In other words, he achieved understanding of the meaning of life. Buddhists say this is a feeling of total peace, when you can stop thinking about yourself and become totally free.

From this time on, Siddattha Gotama was called the Buddha. According to Buddhist teaching, having achieved Enlightenment, Siddattha could have left earth but he chose not to. He believed his knowledge should be passed on to others, so he spent the rest of his life teaching people about the right ways to live. He passed away (Buddhists do not say he died) at the age of 80. His body was **cremated**, and the ashes were placed in special burial mounds called **stupas**. Buddhists say that the Buddha's passing away was when he entered **Parinirvana**. This is the name given to the 'complete' Nirvana after a Buddha's body has stopped living.

▼ *This 'reclining Buddha' statue in Sri Lanka shows the Buddha just before he entered Parinirvana.*

The history of Buddhism

Buddhists believe that there were Buddhas before Gotama and there will be other Buddhas in the future. Therefore they refer to Gotama's teaching as 'the present Buddhist teaching'. This began in India, when Siddattha Gotama reached **Enlightenment**, because he chose to stay in the world to show others the best way to live.

First followers

The Buddha's first followers were the five holy men with whom he had spent years when he was searching for Enlightenment. Before long, other people became interested in his teachings, too, and asked to join him. The group became known as the **Sangha**. The Buddha's first followers included his own son, Rahula. At first, women were not allowed but Gotama was persuaded by his step-mother and his cousin, and eventually he agreed that women, too, could join the group. For 45 years, the Buddha spent his time travelling around India and neighbouring countries, preaching and teaching.

Emperor Asoka

After the Buddha had passed away, his followers carried on his teaching and Buddhism continued to grow. The teaching about respecting all life caught the attention of the Emperor Asoka. He ruled almost the whole of India from 273 BCE to 232 BCE. He had been a keen hunter and soldier, but he became unhappy at the suffering and death he had caused. One day he met a group of Buddhist **monks**. He listened to their teachings and became a Buddhist himself. From then on, he tried to rule according to Buddhist teachings. He encouraged other people to become Buddhists, and sent monks and **nuns** travelling from place to place teaching about Buddhism.

◀ *This pillar was erected by the Emperor Asoka in Delhi, the capital of India, and is made of iron.*

The spread of Buddhism

From India, Buddhism spread to other countries, particularly because of the actions of Asoka. His own son and daughter became a monk and a nun. They took Buddhism to Sri Lanka. By the first century CE it had reached Nepal, Tibet and China, where it grew slowly alongside Chinese religions. By the ninth century it was well established in China, and spreading to neighbouring countries, too. It reached Korea in the fourth century. In Myanmar, (formerly Burma), it was important by the fifth century, and its spread was later helped by the Buddhist ruler Anawratha. From there it spread to Thailand, Cambodia, Malaysia, and Laos. By the sixth century, it was well established in Japan.

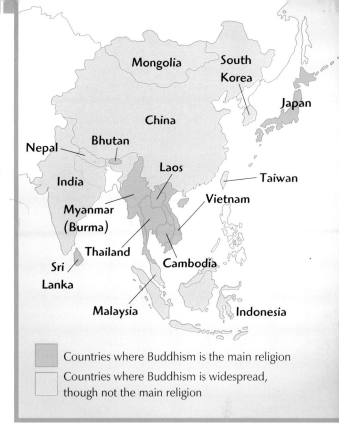

Countries where Buddhism is the main religion

Countries where Buddhism is widespread, though not the main religion

▲ *Countries in the world today where Buddhism is most important.*

Buddhism did not reach Western countries for hundreds of years. In the nineteenth century it travelled from Japan to the Americas, especially to the west coasts. The first Buddhist **missionary** to arrive in England landed in 1893. Today there are Buddhists in almost every country in the world.

As Buddhism spread to different countries, people who became Buddhists did not leave behind everything they had known before. The different groups began to emphasize different teachings. Within a short time, Buddhists had divided into two main groups, **Theravada** and **Mahayana**. Later, other smaller groups emerged, for example, **Tibetan** and **Zen** Buddhists. These groups still exist today. Buddhist customs and particularly festivals are celebrated in quite different ways in different countries.

The Emperor Asoka's columns

Asoka ordered that pillars should be put up, marking where important things had happened to the Buddha, with writing on them explaining what they were. He suggested that people should go on **pilgrimages** to these places. Asoka also had his policies for government written up in the same way. Many of these writings still survive today. They show that Asoka was a conscientious ruler, who took the teachings of the Buddha about caring for others very seriously. For example, one of the tablets called the Rock Edicts reads 'Beloved of the Gods (i.e. Asoka) speaks thus: Father and mother should be respected and so should elders. Kindness to living beings should be made strong and the truth should be spoken. In these ways the **Dhamma** (Buddha's teaching) should be promoted. Likewise a teacher should be honoured by his pupil and proper manners should be shown towards relations. This is an ancient rule that conduces to long life. Thus one should act. Written by the scribe Chapala.'

The main schools of Buddhism

You can find the places mentioned in this book on the map on page 44.

All Buddhists follow the teachings of the Buddha, but different groups do not follow them in exactly the same way. As Buddhism spread, it was influenced by religions which already existed in the countries to which it went. So the ways in which Buddhism was practised became different. In Buddhism, the main groups are known as 'schools'. There are two main schools. One is **Theravada** Buddhism, the other is **Mahayana** Buddhism. Both of these schools have smaller groups. One of the most important groups within Mahayana Buddhism is the Vajrayana ('Diamond Vehicle') School, which is most important in Tibet.

Theravada Buddhism

Theravada means 'teachings of the elders'. Elders are respected leaders of a religion. Theravada Buddhist teachings are written in the language called **Pali**. Today, these are mainly read by **monks**. Theravada is sometimes called 'southern Buddhism' because it is mainly found in Sri Lanka, Myanmar (Burma), Cambodia, Thailand and Vietnam.

Theravada Buddhists emphasize the idea that each person must gain **Enlightenment** for themselves. No one else can do it for you. They believe that the Buddha taught people how they should live, but he was only a man. The only way he can help people to gain Enlightenment today is through his teachings, so Theravada Buddhists do not pray to the Buddha.

Theravada Buddhists think that the best way to live is as a monk. A monk can concentrate on his religion, because he has no responsibilities, such as family, or possessions. Women can become **nuns**, and live in the same way as monks, although they do not follow exactly the same rules. Not everyone can leave their home and dedicate their life to their religion, and Theravada Buddhists accept that this means monks and nuns may be closer to Nirvana than other people. Because of the importance that they attach to monks and nuns, Theravada Buddhists believe that it is an important part of their religious duty to give food and other gifts to the monks and **monasteries**.

◄ *A typical Theravada Buddharupa (statue of Buddha) is serene and calm.*

Mahayana Buddhism

Mahayana Buddhism began in India in about 100 BCE. It is now more popular in the 'northern' countries of China, Japan, Korea and Tibet and among Buddhists in some Western countries. It includes many different smaller schools. Mahayana Buddhism follows the same ideas as Theravada Buddhism, but in some cases it has changed the way they are understood and explained. Mahayana means 'great vehicle'. This is a way of saying that there is room for different ways to **Nirvana**.

▲ *A typical Mahayana Buddharupa is jolly and smiling.*

Bodhisattvas

Belief in **Bodhisattvas** is an important difference between Theravada and Mahayana Buddhists. According to Mahayana Buddhist belief, a Bodhisattva is someone who is destined to reach Enlightenment, but has postponed actually achieving it so that they can stay in the world to help others to achieve Enlightenment, too. This is a sign of how much they care about other people. Caring for others is a very important part of Buddhist teaching. There are many thousands of Bodhisattvas. Mahayana Buddhists pray to them for help in achieving Enlightenment, and also for help with problems in everyday life.

Both Theravada and Mahayana Buddhists use statues (rupas) of the Buddha to help them in their worship. As a general rule, Theravada rupas show a Buddha who is calm, serious and serene. Some Mahayana Buddhist rupas are jolly and smiling.

The Three Jewels

All Buddhists believe that the most important statements of Buddhist belief can be summed up in the Three Jewels, sometimes called the Three Gems. They were given this name because Buddhists believe that they are the most precious part of their belief.

I take refuge in the Buddha (The Enlightened One)
*I take refuge in the **Dhamma** (Teaching)*
*I take refuge in the **Sangha** (the Buddhist community)*

A refuge is somewhere that is safe, so when Buddhists say that they take refuge, they are showing that these things are something that they can put at the centre of their lives.

Schools of Mahayana Buddhism

There are many different schools in **Mahayana** Buddhism. Each one has its own particular beliefs and ways of practising. As a general rule, Mahayana Buddhists are less likely to become **monks** and **nuns**. They believe that lay people (non-monks and nuns) are equally important.

▲ *Zen Buddhist monks spend many hours each day meditating.*

Zen Buddhism

Zen is a Japanese word which means **meditation**. Zen Buddhism is most popular in Japan and Korea, and in China where it is called Cha'an. Like all Buddhists, followers of Zen Buddhism aim to reach **Enlightenment**. Zen Buddhists say that you cannot reach Enlightenment by thinking about it – you have to go beyond your mind to achieve it. The idea is not that you can make something happen if it is not there, but that people are capable of a higher understanding if they 'wake up' to it.

Zen Buddhists have their own ways of trying to reach Enlightenment, and say that it comes as a flash of higher understanding. The majority of their time is spent in Za-Zen, that is, sitting in meditation. The idea is to shock your mind out of its usual ways of thought, into understanding.

Pure Land Buddhism

Pure Land (Jodo Shin Shu) Buddhism is particularly popular in Japan. It also has many followers in the United States. It teaches that this age of the world is so wicked that people cannot achieve **Nirvana** on their own. The only hope is to pray to the Buddha Amida, Lord of the Pure Land. The Pure Land is **Sukhavati**, a sort of paradise full of fruit and flowers. Pure Land Buddhists teach that this is a stage on the way to Nirvana, but it is a very different idea from the **Theravada** teaching about Nirvana as an extinguishing of all the desires of life. A **mantra** used by followers of this school is called the Nembutsu, 'Nemu Amida Butsu', which means 'Praise the Amida Buddha'. The ideas of the Pure Land school are not accepted by many other Buddhists, who feel that they do not follow the teachings of the Buddha Gotama.

Tibetan Buddhism

Tibetan Buddhists have their own **shrines** and way of worship. They hold the greatest respect for their leader the **Dalai Lama**. They believe he is an appearance of the **Bodhisattva** Chenresi, who is most important for Tibetans. There is a mantra which is like a prayer to this Bodhisattva. It is *'Aum mane padme hum'*. In English this is 'Glory to the jewel in the lotus' but its true meaning cannot really be translated. The prayer is written on prayer wheels and prayer flags.

Prayer wheels are cylinders, usually made of bronze, with a prayer written on special paper rolled up in the centre. They can be small enough to hold, but many temples have huge prayer wheels. The larger the wheel, the more powerful the prayer. As the wheels are turned and the flags blow in the wind, Tibetan Buddhists believe the prayer is repeated over and over. The prayers are a way of building up **merit**, the reward for doing good things.

Mudras (hand gestures) and **mandalas** (special patterns) are also important for Tibetan Buddhists. They believe they can help you on your way to Nirvana.

In 1959, the Chinese took over Tibet. They did not approve of Buddhist practices, and many **monasteries** and Buddhist monuments were destroyed. Thousands of Tibetans were killed in demonstrations. The Dalai Lama now lives in exile in Dharmsala in northern India.

▲ *A prayer wheel in a Tibetan Buddhist monastery.*

A Zen story

There is a Zen Buddhist story about a young trainee in a **monastery**. He sat for a whole day in the **lotus position**. At last, the master appeared and asked him what he was doing. He said that he was trying to become a Buddha. The master picked up a stone and began to polish it. Curious, the young man asked what he was doing. 'Making a mirror' replied the master. The trainee said, 'But you can't make a mirror out of a stone'. 'Neither can any amount of sitting cross-legged make you a Buddha', said the master.

What the Buddha taught

You can find the places mentioned in this book on the map on page 44.

Most Buddhists agree that the **Buddha's** teaching can be summed up in three parts. The first is the Three Signs of Being, the second is the Four Noble Truths and the third is the Noble Eightfold Path. Buddhists believe that, taken together, these three teachings show the best ways to live.

The Three Signs of Being

The three signs of being can be summed up in three words – **dukkha**, **anicca** and **anatta**.

Dukkha is often translated as 'suffering', but it means more than that. Anything which is less than perfect is dukkha – which means everything in the world. The best translation is probably 'unsatisfactoriness'. The Buddha said that everything in life was dukkha. Anicca means 'impermanence' – nothing lasts. Everything, even 'solid' things like mountains, are always changing. Buddhists believe that the only escape from this continual change is **Nirvana**. Anatta means 'no soul'. The Buddha said that there is no such thing as a soul or a spirit. Each person has a body, thoughts, feelings, ideas and awareness. These five parts, and the way they come together, make up each person. When a body dies, the parts fall apart and are re-assembled in a different way to make another person. What continues from one life to the next is **kamma** (the 'life-force') which a person creates while they are alive. The force of a good life will lead to a 'higher' life next time. The force of a bad life will lead to a 'lower' life next time.

▲ Buddhists believe that everything in life is dukkha – unsatisfactory – but everyone should work to the best of their ability.

What the Buddha said

The best of paths is the path of eight; the best of truths the four sayings. The best of states, freedom from passions. The best of men, the one who sees. This is the path, there is no other that leads to visions. Whoever goes on this path travels to the end of sorrow.

(Dhammapada 20: 273-6)

The Four Noble Truths

In his first sermon after he had achieved **Enlightenment**, the Buddha preached to the five holy men with whom he had spent several years searching for the meaning of life. This took place at Sarnath, the Deer Park in Varanasi. Buddhists generally agree that the most important part of this sermon was the teaching called the Four Noble Truths. They are based around dukkha.

▲ *Pilgrims at Sarnath, in Varansi, India, where the Buddha preached his first sermon on the Four Noble Truths.*

- *Life is dukkha.*
  Everything in life is dukkha (unsatisfactory), because nothing in this world is perfect. The only release from dukkha is to achieve Nirvana.

- *Dukkha is caused by greed and desire.*
  Everyone is basically selfish – we all think more about ourselves than others, and want to do what we want rather than what others want.

- *Greed and selfishness can be overcome.*
  Breaking out of the rebirth cycle can be achieved by gaining Nirvana, which is freedom from all desires.

- *The way to overcome this cycle is the Noble Eightfold Path.*

The Noble Eightfold Path

The Noble Eightfold Path shows the Middle Way between extremes, which Buddhists should follow in their lives. 'Right' means 'best possible'– that is, using Buddhist teachings. All of these things need to be acted on together.

- *Right viewpoint*
  Looking at life in the right way, and following the basic teachings of Buddhism.

- *Right thought*
  Using your mind in the right way so that you become unselfish.

- *Right speech*
  Being kind and helpful when you talk to people, and not tell lies, swear or gossip.

- *Right action*
  Avoiding killing, stealing or being dishonest. Being faithful to your husband or wife, not drinking alcohol or taking non-medicinal drugs.

- *Right living*
  Working to the best of your ability. The job you do should be useful, and not involve anything which harms others.

- *Right effort*
  Avoiding bad things and working hard to do good.

- *Right awareness*
  Controlling your mind so that you can see things around you in the right way.

- *Right concentration*
  Training your mind by meditation to concentrate without wandering.

The holy books

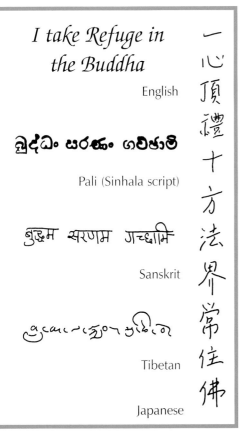

I take Refuge in the Buddha

English

 බුද්ධං සරණං ගච්ඡාමි

Pali (Sinhala script)

बुद्धम् सरणम् गच्छामि

Sanskrit

 སངས་རྒྱས་ལ་སྐྱབས་སུ་མཆིའོ།

Tibetan

一心頂禮十方法界常住佛

Japanese

▲ *The Buddhist books are written in several languages.*

At first, none of the Buddha's teachings were written down. At the time when he was alive, not many people could read and write, so they were far more used to remembering things. However, soon after he had passed away, people began to think that it would be a good idea to make sure there was a clear record of what the Buddha had said. All his followers knew the most important teachings, but few people knew everything that he had taught. Since his teachings were thought to be so important, a written record of all of them was necessary.

A special meeting of 500 Buddhist **monks** was arranged. All the Buddha's teaching was recited by the **Venerable** Ananda and the Venerable Upali, who were two of the Buddha's closest followers. (Venerable is a title which is often used by Buddhists for **monks**. It means someone who is very respected.) All the monks repeated the teaching together. This made sure that everyone agreed. This teaching was passed down by the monks. It was not written down for about 400 years, but in that time there were several meetings to check that it was still accurate and to organize it.

The two canons

The two most important collections of the Buddha's teaching are called the **Pali Canon** and the **Sanskrit** Canon. A canon is a collection of writings. It comes from the Greek word for a ruler used for measuring, and is the word used in most religions to describe the holy books that are accepted as genuine. Pali and Sanskrit are the ancient languages in which the collections of teaching were made. The Pali canon was written down first. It is also called the **Tipitaka**, which means 'three baskets'. It was probably given this name because the teachings were first written down on palm leaves, which were kept in baskets. In the days before paper was common, it was common for leaves to be used instead. The leaf was flattened, and then the words were etched (carved) into the leaves with a metal stylus. A stylus is like a pen with a sharp point which is used to scratch patterns. The leaf was then rubbed over with carbon ink, so that the pattern of the etching was filled, and the letters showed up. The first two baskets of the Tipitaka contain the most important teachings for all Buddhists. **Theravada** and **Mahayana** Buddhists have different ideas about what should be included in the third basket.

Mahayana Buddhist books

As well as the Buddha's teachings, which all Buddhists accept, Mahayana Buddhists also have teachings which are particularly important to different groups. An important document for all Mahayana Buddhists is the **Lotus sutra**. There are also many documents in languages other than Sanskrit and Pali which form part of the teachings of different schools of Mahayana Buddhists. For **Tibetan** Buddhism, the Ka-guyur text is one of its most important collections of teaching. This has 108 volumes of teaching and 225 more volumes which explain the teachings.

In China, there are reckoned to be 1662 different teachings, of which the most important is the **Diamond Sutra**, which dates from the fourth century CE. Many of the teachings were engraved on polished stone and rocks, and can still be seen today. Some were written on dark blue paper, using gold or silver ink. In about the eighth century CE, Chinese Buddhists had the idea of carving mirror images of Chinese characters onto wooden blocks so that they could be used to print several copies of the sutras. This was how wood-block printing started. A copy of the Diamond Sutra, printed by this method in 868 CE, still exists today.

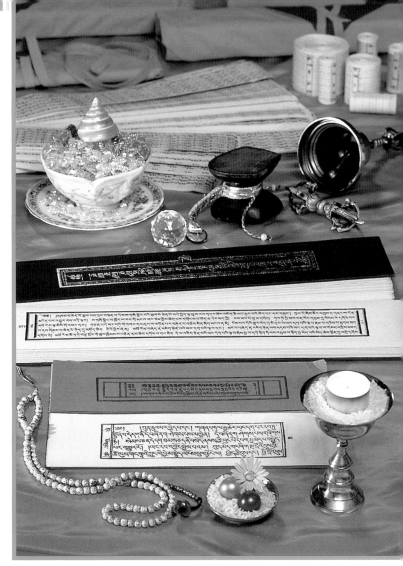

▲ *Like the individual leaves on which they were first written down, Buddhist teachings are still written on separate pieces of paper.*

The two canons

From a very early stage Buddhist Scriptures were written in two languages. This is the reason why many important Buddhist words can be spelled two ways. For example, the state that Buddhists are trying to achieve can be called **Nirvana** or **Nibbana**. Nirvana is the Sanskrit form, Nibbana is the Pali form of the word. **Sutta** is the Pali form of the word for a small piece of teaching, Sutra is the Sanskrit form. Neither form is 'better' or 'more correct' than the other. In this book, the Pali form is the one which is used more often, e.g. Dhamma, not Dharma.

Buddhist teachings – what the holy books say

The most important Buddhist teachings are the **Tipitaka**, the three baskets. Almost all Buddhists agree on the contents of the first two baskets, but **Mahayana** Buddhists have their own teachings in the third basket which are different from the teachings which **Theravada** Buddhists include.

▲ *Young Buddhist monks reading the Scriptures at a **monastery** in India.*

The Tipitaka

The first 'basket' of the Tipitaka is called the Vinaya Pitaka, which means 'discipline'. It contains the rules for **monks** to follow, with some stories and other teachings. The second 'basket' is the **Sutta** Pitaka, which contains most of the **dhamma**, the teachings of the **Buddha**. The third 'basket' is the Abhidhamma Pitaka, which means 'higher teaching'. Most of this basket consists of writings which explain the Buddha's teaching.

The most important of these three baskets is the Sutta Pitaka, because it contains the teachings of the Buddha. A sutta is a small piece of teaching. A well-known part of this basket is called the Dhammapada, which contains the most memorable sayings of the Buddha. Buddhists spend a lot of time studying these words. The most important part is the section called the Path of Teaching, because this contains the Four Noble Truths and The Noble Eightfold Path. The Sutta Pitaka also contains stories about the Buddha, including stories about his previous lives before he was Gotama.

Quotations from the holy books

The reason why Buddhists believe that the holy books are so important can be seen in these quotes from the Buddha:

If you really want to see me, look at my teaching.
(Samyutta Nikaya)

Just before he passed away, the Buddha said to his companion the **Venerable** Ananda:

When I am gone, do not say that you have no teacher. Whatever I have taught, let that be your teacher when I am gone.
(Mahaparinibbana Sutta – a **Pali** teaching)

Much of the Buddha's teaching was about the importance of behaving in the right way. The first quotation below is from the Sanskrit Sutra of the Forty-two Chapters. This is believed to have been the first sutra to be translated into Chinese, when it was organized so that the teaching was in forty-two sections.

The Buddha said,
For human beings, ten things are evil. Three are of the body; four are of the mouth; and the other three are of the mind. The three evils of the body are needless killing, stealing and sensual misconduct. The four evils of the mouth are saying one thing but meaning another, slander, lying and improper language. The three evils of the mind are greed, anger and foolishness.

Who is tactful and energetic,
And gains wealth by his own effort,
He will acquire fame by truth,
And friendship by giving.

He who has faith and is also truthful,
Virtuous, firm and fond of giving;
By virtue of these four conditions
Will never in the hereafter feel sorry.

Truth and Restraint,
Charity and Forbearance,
Are the greatest reformers of
human beings.
(Alavaka Sutta)

▲ *Worshipping at the feet of a* **Buddharupa** *in Thailand.*

Hold not a sin of little worth, thinking 'this is little to me'. The falling of drops of water will in time fill a jar of water. Even so the foolish man becomes full of evil, although he gather it little by little.

Hold not a deed of little worth, thinking 'this is little to me.' The falling of drops of water will in time fill a jar. Even so, the wise man becomes full of good, although he gather it little by little.
(Dhammapada 9: 121–2)

Symbols in Buddhism

The teachings of Buddhism include many ideas that are difficult to explain. Using symbols helps to make things clear. It also means that ideas can be explained without using words, which is useful when teachings are being translated into another language. The lotus flower, for example, is often used as a symbol for Buddhism. Flowers are often used as offerings at Buddhist **shrines**. They help to make the shrine attractive and they smell pleasant. However, they soon decay and die, which makes them a symbol of the belief that nothing lasts.

The Buddha

There are thousands of **Buddharupas** (images of the Buddha), in countries all over the world. They use many symbols. The Buddha is usually shown in one of three positions – standing, sitting or lying down. His hands are in different positions, showing an aspect of his teaching. If he is standing, he usually has the right hand raised with the palm outward, showing he is blessing people. The left hand is extended, in a gesture showing that he is giving. In some other statues, he is standing with both hands in front of his chest, palms together. This is the usual Indian gesture which shows both greeting and respect.

When the Buddharupa is sitting down, he is often in the **lotus position**, meditating. If he is teaching, he is usually sitting with one hand raised. The hand positions are called **mudras**. Sometimes the first finger of his left hand is pointing to his right hand, and the thumb and first finger of his right hand form a circle. This is called 'Setting the Wheel of Law in motion'. It is a reference to his first teaching, when he talked about the wheel of the laws of life. Sometimes his right hand is touching the earth. This refers to the story about the evil spirit Mara tempting him while he was **meditating**. The story tells that Mara told the Buddha his **Enlightenment** was not real, and that even if it was he would do better to enter **Nirvana** straight away rather than remain on earth to teach others. The Buddha's reply was to touch the earth, calling it to witness that there have always been people who have spent their lives trying to help others.

◀ *This statue of the Buddha at Sukhothal in Thailand shows the Buddha meditating. Notice the lotus flowers in the water, another Buddhist symbol.*

Pictures and images of the Buddha lying down show him at the end of his life, just before he entered **Parinirvana**. They usually show him as very serene and calm.

Whatever the position, Buddharupas may show any or all of 32 special symbols which show that the Buddha was not an ordinary person. For example, there is usually a bump on the top of this head, which is a sign that he had special gifts. He is often shown with a round mark on his forehead, sometimes called a 'third eye'. No one suggests that Gotama really had this, but it is a symbol that he could see things which ordinary people cannot see. He is usually shown with long ear lobes, showing that he came from an important family. His hair is usually curled, a symbol that he was a very holy man.

Mandalas

A **mandala** is a specially designed pattern made up of circles, squares and triangles. The Wheel of the Law (the wheel with eight spokes which shows the Noble Eightfold Path) is a mandala. Sometimes they are just patterns, but they may include pictures of the Buddha or of **Bodhisattvas**. Some show stages of life and animals. They, too, are symbols, for example, a snake stands for hatred, a cockerel for greed and a pig for ignorance. Mandalas show Buddhist teachings and are used to help Buddhists meditate.

▶ *A mandala is a specially designed pattern to help Buddhists meditate.*

Lalini's view

Lalini is 15 and lives in Sri Lanka.

Not far from where I live there is a very famous statue of the Buddha at a temple called Buddhurajamaha Vihara. My father told me it's 50 metres high – I worked out a long time ago that this means it's 27 times taller then he is! The statue sits at the edge of a park, on a special platform. The Buddha is sitting down, meditating in the lotus position. He has his eyes closed and looks very peaceful. His robes are painted bright yellow. I like just going to look at it, to remember what the Buddha taught. He looks very kind, and he taught people to be kind to others. I try, but it's hard, sometimes!

Ways of worship

Buddhists may worship on their own or in groups. There is no special day of the week when they meet for worship, but days before the moon is new, full or at half-moon are important. Many Buddhists believe that the Buddha was born, gained **Enlightenment** and passed away on days when the moon was full.

Shrines

Buddhists usually worship in front of a **shrine**. A shrine is a special place which is considered to be holy by followers of a religion because of what it contains. Buddhist shrines are beautifully decorated, and always contain an image of the Buddha, a **Buddharupa**. Buddhist shrines also contain holders for **incense**, a spice which burns with a strong, sweet smell. There are usually flowers and candles, with places where offerings can be left. Different Buddhist schools have different traditions about other things which may be found in shrines – for example, **Zen** Buddhist shrines may have offerings of tea, **Tibetan** Buddhist shrines have bowls of water in them.

Shrine rooms may also be quite different. In Zen Buddhism, the rooms are usually very plain and simple. In other traditions the room may be highly decorated with paintings, candles and statues. A shrine may be the central point of a **monastery** or temple, or it may be one room or part of a room in an ordinary house. This is more likely in countries where there are not many Buddhist temples. Some Buddhists, but not all, have shrines in their own homes.

Individual worship

When they worship on their own, Buddhists **meditate** and chant parts of the holy books. (Chanting is a special sort of singing, using only a few notes.) They often burn incense, and offer flowers and sometimes food, such as grains of rice, to the Buddharupa. They may light candles, a symbol of the light of the Buddha's teaching. **Theravada** Buddhists do not pray as part of their worship, but **Mahayana** Buddhists pray to **Bodhisattvas** for help.

◀ *A Tibetan Buddhist's shrine at their home in the UK.*

Group worship

When Buddhists meet for worship, it is usually in the shrine room of a temple. Before they go into the shrine room, worshippers remove their shoes. This is to show respect as well as to keep the room clean for worship. There are no seats, so worshippers sit on the floor. Pointing the legs towards the image is disrespectful, so they are kept crossed or pointing to one side. Worshippers may greet the Buddharupa in the shrine by putting their hands together in front of their chest or face, and bowing slightly. This is the usual way of greeting anyone in many Eastern countries. Sometimes a Buddhist touches their chest, lips and forehead with their hands, to show that their body, their speech and their mind are all joining in the greeting. They may bow or kneel, and sometimes lie flat on the floor. These are all ways of showing respect to the image.

▲ The shrine in the temple at Sarnath in India, built where the Buddha preached his first sermon.

The people offer gifts of flowers and light (by lighting candles or lamps). In a temple, **monks** usually carry out the formal parts of the ceremonies. The people watch and meditate, and repeat set words and chants after the monks. There are readings from the Buddhist holy books, and a senior monk often gives a talk. At the end of the ceremony, the people often stay and drink tea together. Tea-drinking ceremonies can be part of worship. The people sit quietly, drinking specially prepared tea from beautiful crockery. There are often flower arrangements. The idea is to be surrounded by peace and beauty.

Meditation

For most Buddhists, meditation is the most important part of worship. Meditation is intended to control, develop and train the mind so that you can focus on things that are really important. The point of meditation is to 'rise above' any worries you may have, and the world and its problems. Buddhists usually sit on the floor, often with crossed legs, and focus on an object. This may be a Buddharupa or a beautiful object such as a flower. Sometimes they focus on a **mantra** instead. They try to empty their mind of all other thoughts. Then they concentrate on an idea of formlessness. With practice, they cease to have to concentrate and can experience a sense of peace and inner joy. Buddhists believe that by meditating, they will become better people, and will be able to achieve Enlightenment.

Buddhist monks and nuns

▲ *Young monks relaxing in the grounds of their monastery.*

The first Order (community) of Buddhist **monks** was begun by the Buddha. At first he would not allow women followers, but he later gave permission for Orders of **nuns**. Today, monks (**bhikkhus**) and nuns (**bhikkhunis**) live in the same way, although the rules they follow are not always exactly the same. There are many more monks than nuns.

Monks live in a **monastery**, usually called a **vihara**. A vihara is often like a small village. Many are built around a **stupa** or important temple. The most important room is the **shrine** room, used for worship and important meetings of the monks. Many Buddhists who live near a vihara go there to worship or study, and children go to school there, to be taught by the monks. In **Theravada** Buddhist countries, young boys often become monks so that they can be educated in the vihara. They may leave when they become adult. Sometimes Buddhist men become monks for a few months or years, to study and learn more about Buddhism. It is not expected that all monks will stay in the vihara all their lives.

Life in the vihara

The monks spend most of the day alone, studying and meditating. The Buddha taught that helping others is important, so many monks spend part of their day teaching, giving advice to people, or helping in some other way. They eat their main meal before midday, and then **fast** until the following morning, although they may drink water, or tea without milk or sugar.

A vihara has small huts or rooms where monks live alone. These are furnished very simply, with a mat as the monk's bed, and a small table. He is expected to sit on the floor. There may also be a small shrine to help the monk **meditate**. Anything which is not essential – for example, pens, paper or books – belongs to the vihara. The only things which a monk owns himself are the robe he wears – most monks have two – and a few necessary items. These are a needle and thread to repair the robes, a razor, because most monks shave their heads, a bowl and cup for food and drink, and a special strainer. This is to remove any insects from his drinking water. Buddhists try not to kill anything, even by accident.

The five precepts

All Buddhists are expected to follow the five **precepts**, which are the guides for living as a Buddhist. The five precepts are:

- not to harm living beings
- not to take what is not given
- to avoid improper sexual activity
- not to take part in improper speech
- to avoid alcohol and the misuse of drugs.

When a Buddhist becomes a monk or nun, these rules are followed more strictly – for example, a Buddhist monk should never be alone with a woman. There are also five extra precepts which all monks and nuns and some other Buddhists choose to follow. They agree:

- not to eat after midday
- not to attend music or dancing
- not to use perfume or jewellery
- not to sleep on a comfortable bed
- not to accept gifts of money.

There are also rules of the vihara which monks and nuns must keep.

▲ *These Buddhist nuns are worshipping at a temple in Myanmar (Burma).*

Alms

Monks are given food and everything else they need by people living around the vihara. This is called giving **alms**. Giving to monks is part of a Buddhist's religious duty, which helps to earn **merit**. Monks used to go out collecting alms every morning, but today people usually take gifts to the vihara.

Stupas

A stupa is a burial mound or building. The first stupas were built over the places where parts of the Buddha's ashes were buried after his body had been **cremated**. The ashes were divided into eight equal parts, and buried in major Indian cities. A stupa was built at the place where the body had been burned and another where the container which had held the ashes was buried. This gave ten stupas altogether. Later, other stupas were built to honour the remains of important Buddhists, or where other important **relics** were buried. Although their design varies in different countries, stupas are usually built to a symbolic pattern. A mound represents the four elements, air, earth, fire, water and a tower or spire represents wisdom.

Buddhist worship around the world

▲ *The Shwe Dagon Pagoda in Rangoon is the oldest Buddhist temple in Myanmar (Burma).*

The Shwe Dagon Pagoda, Rangoon, Myanmar (Burma)

'Pagoda' is the name for a particular shape of Buddhist temple. The Shwe Dagon pagoda is the oldest Buddhist temple in Myanmar, and one of the most important in the world. Eight hairs from the Buddha's head were brought there 2500 years ago, and are still treasured.

The pagoda itself (the pointed section at the centre of the temple) stands 100 metres (325 feet) high. The temple was given its present form by King Shinbyusim in 1774, when he covered the pagoda in his own weight in gold. The huge *hti* (umbrella – the decoration at the highest point of the pagoda which is a symbol of **Nirvana**) includes 1500 bells, one hundred of them gold, the rest silver. The pagoda itself is approached by four covered staircases, one at each main point of the compass. These lead to a marble walkway which surrounds the base of the pagoda. There are places where flowers can be offered, and the whole place throngs with tourists and pilgrims.

You can find the places mentioned in this book on the map on page 44.

The Swayambunath stupa, Kathmandu, Nepal

Swayambunath is built on a hill overlooking the Kathmandu valley. It is reached by climbing 300 steps up from the valley. It has been a centre of worship and **pilgrimage** for 2500 years, and is supposed to have been visited by the Emperor Asoka in the second century BCE.

Swayambunath follows the symbolic pattern of all Buddhist **stupas**, so the mound represents the four elements. In this stupa the spire consists of thirteen rings covered in gold, which represent the thirteen degrees of knowledge, rising like a ladder to Nirvana, represented by the umbrella at the top. Above the umbrella is a golden **vajra** (symbolic thunderbolt) which is a common Buddhist symbol, representing the way **Enlightenment** comes like a bolt of lightning. On all four sides of the stupa, painted eyes represent the all-seeing eyes of Buddha. The 'nose' between them is a Nepalese number one, a symbol of unity.

Around the base of the stupa are huge prayer wheels, which are turned by Buddhists as part of their worship.

The Chuang Yen Monastery, USA

The Chuang Yen **Monastery** is just outside New York. It is a centre for following the teachings of the **Pure Land** School of Buddhism. The central part of the monastery is the Hall of Ten Thousand Buddhas, which can seat up to 2000 people. It contains an image of the Buddha which is 11.2 metres (37 feet) high. This is the largest statue of the Buddha in the western hemisphere. It took eight years to construct, and is so large that the hall had to be built around it. Surrounding the building is a terrace which has 10,000 small statues of the Buddha as part of a mural. Another important room in the monastery is the Kuan-Yin room. Kuan Yin is an important **Bodhisattva** for Pure Land Buddhists and the room contains two rare statues of her. One, made of porcelain, is almost 700 years old. The other, made of wood, is almost 2 metres tall and is thought to be over 1000 years old. The monastery is home to a group of **monks** and **nuns**, who organize **retreats** for Buddhists, as well as teaching, study camps and other activities.

▲ The Chuang-Yen monastery, near New York, has the largest statue of the Buddha in the western hemisphere.

Buddhist teaching

This quotation comes from teaching by Phra Ajahan Yantra Amaro, a modern Buddhist teacher. The **Dhamma** is the Buddha's teaching which all Buddhists try to follow.

Hold a little smile within your heart.
For loving kindness gives the world a peaceful shelter.
Righteousness is Dhamma.
One-ness of heart is the seat of all nature:
All Dhamma rises from the one-ness of heart.

Pilgrimage

Pilgrimages are journeys that are made for religious reasons. People have many different reasons for going on pilgrimages. For Buddhists, the main reason is that they believe going to holy places, especially places where the Buddha lived and worked, will help them in their own search for **Enlightenment**. They may also visit places such as the **stupas** where part of the Buddha's ashes were buried, or famous and important temples. There are sixteen sites of pilgrimage for Buddhists, of which four are believed to be the most important. These are the four places which the Buddha said his followers should visit.

You can find the places mentioned in this book on the map on page 44.

Lumbini

The Buddha was born at Lumbini, in what is now south-western Nepal. The site where he was born is marked by a simple stone pillar which says on it 'Here the Buddha was born'. This pillar was erected by the Emperor Asoka in 250 BCE, and only rediscovered in 1895. Lumbini is now quite a difficult place to get to, but a small group of **monks** live there, and there are temples where people meditate. An ancient **shrine** marks the very spot where the Buddha is said to have been born in a palace garden.

Bodh Gaya

Bodh Gaya is 100 km (62 miles) south of Patna, in India. It is the place where the Buddha gained Enlightenment. Buddhists from all over the world visit it, and it is an important meeting place. Many different Buddhist traditions have temples there, built in the traditional architectures of the countries from which they come. On the western side of the temple is a **bodhi tree**, said to be descended from the very tree under which the Buddha sat to **meditate**. Close to the tree is a red sandstone slab which Buddhists believe is the stone on which the Buddha sat. Under the tree are carvings of the Buddha's footprints, where pilgrims may lay flowers. They may walk around the tree, their heads and feet bare as a sign of respect, and they often sit under it to meditate. The main temple at the site is called the Mahabodhi temple. It has a central tower 52 metres (160 feet) high. Inside is a **Buddharupa** (image of the Buddha) covered in gold leaf.

◀ *Pilgrims at Bodh Gaya in India, where the Buddha gained Enlightenment.*

Sarnath

Sarnath is the place just north of Varanasi, in India, where the Buddha preached his first sermon after he had gained Enlightenment. It was the place where Asoka erected one of the finest pillars marking a site of importance to Buddhists (see page 9). The capital (top piece) of this pillar has four lion heads, and is in the museum there.

Kushinagara

The Buddha passed away at Kushinagara in northern India, and many Buddhists visit the stupa there. The Kushinara **Nirvana** temple was built in 1956, to make it easier for pilgrims to walk around (circumambulate) the stupa. When visiting a stupa, a Buddhist walks around it at least three times. This recalls the Three Refuges (the **Dhamma**, the Buddha and the **Sangha**). Inside the temple is a red stone statue, six metres long, of the reclining Buddha, showing him just before he entered **Parinirvana**. The statue is believed to be 1500 years old. It was restored in the nineteenth century.

▼ *Sri Pada, near Kandy, on the island of Sri Lanka, is a very special place for Buddhists because they believe the Buddha visited it.*

Other important places

Buddhists may visit many other sites in India and neighbouring countries on pilgrimage. For example, on the island of Sri Lanka is a mountain called Sri Pada, the Sacred Peak. Buddhists believe that the Buddha visited Sri Lanka three times, and went once to Sri Pada. At the top of the mountain is a stone which has what look like footprints on it. Buddhists believe that these footprints were left by the Buddha.

About pilgrimage

According to a fifteenth-century **Tibetan** commentary on the Vinaya Sutra, the Buddha taught that pilgrimage was very important.

*'**Bhikkhus**, after my passing away, all sons and daughters who are of good family and are faithful should as long as they live, go to the four holy places and remember: here at Lumbini the enlightened one was born; here at Bodh Gaya he attained Enlightenment; here at Sarnath he turned the wheel of Dhamma; and there at Kushinagar he entered Parinirvana … After my passing away, the new bhikkhus who come and ask of the doctrine should be told of these four places and advised that a pilgrimage to them will help purify their previously accumulated **Kammas** or actions.'*

Celebrations – Wesak and Hana Matsuri

Wesak

The Buddhist year follows the cycles of the moon, not the sun. This is called a lunar year. It is shorter than a year which runs by the position of the sun. Buddhist festivals are held on full moon days. The most important is the full moon day in the month of Wesak, which falls in May or June in the Western calendar. According to **Theravada** Buddhist teaching, this is the day when the Buddha was born, achieved **Enlightenment** and passed away. Although the festival has different names in different countries, it is celebrated by Buddhists all over the world.

Western countries (Buddha Day)

In Britain and other English-speaking countries, the festival of Wesak is often called Buddha Day. Buddhists go to a temple or monastery and listen to a talk by the monks about the Buddha's life and his Enlightenment. They often chant and **meditate**, sometimes for the whole night. Many Buddhists give each other cards and presents to celebrate the festival. The temple is decorated with flowers and streamers, and it is a very joyful occasion.

◀ *Buddha Day celebrations are important for Buddhists in many Western countries.*

Sam's view

Sam is 11 and lives with his parents in California.

We always go to the temple on Buddha Day. There are lots of people there, and we all sit on the floor and listen while a monk gives us a talk about the Buddha and his teaching. Everyone sits and meditates. I'm still learning how to meditate – it's really hard, because I suddenly find I'm thinking about playing soccer with the kids at school. Then I have to try to concentrate all over again. It is easier at the temple, because I can sit and look at the Buddharupa. He looks calm and peaceful, and I try to remember his teaching. For me, the best bit of Buddha Day is the meal at the temple!

Sri Lanka

In Sri Lanka, special ceremonies and worship take place in the temples. Streets and temples are lit with huge lanterns, with paintings on them showing scenes from the Buddha's life. People make similar small lanterns to decorate their houses. There are plays and dancing. Part of Wesak is having a good time and enjoying yourself, but the real meaning of the festival is to remember the Buddha's teaching. He taught that it is very important to be kind and generous to all living things, so everyone makes a special effort to be kind to others. Many people dress in white clothes, and take gifts of flowers to the **monasteries**. This is to remind everyone what the Buddha taught.

Thailand (Vaisakha)

People in Thailand visit temples and monasteries, where **monks** give talks and preach to people about the life of the Buddha. The **shrines** in the temples are beautifully decorated. A special part of the festival is when the people pour scented water over the **Buddharupa**, the image of the Buddha. At night, the image is taken out of the temple and put on a special platform. People go to the monastery with lighted candles or lamps, and carry flowers and **incense** sticks. They walk around the Buddharupa three times. This is to remember the Three Jewels – once for the Buddha, once for the **Dhamma** (teaching), and once for the **Sangha** (community). The Buddharupa is therefore surrounded by light and sweet scent.

Hana Matsuri

Mahayana Buddhist countries celebrate the birth of the Buddha in April, his Enlightenment in December and his passing away in February. Hana Matsuri ('Flower festival') takes place in Japan to celebrate the birth of the Buddha. It is a spring festival, and people visiting shrines take offerings of spring flowers. People set up stalls and sell food, and there is traditional dancing. Acrobats often perform in the streets. Displays are set up in the grounds of temples to remind people of stories about the Buddha's birth. Statues of the infant Buddha are decorated with flowers. Children may pour scented tea over the statues, as a reminder of the story that when he was born, two streams of perfumed water appeared from the sky, bathing Gotama and his mother.

▶ *Pouring scented tea over the statues of the Buddha is a traditional part of the celebrations for Hana Matsuri.*

Celebrations – Kathina and Songkran

Kathina

Kathina is a **Theravada** Buddhist festival. It is most important in the countries of Sri Lanka, Myanmar and Thailand. Kathina means 'difficult', and is a reminder that living as a **monk** or **nun** and following the Buddha's teaching is not easy.

▲ *A procession to give cloth for robes to the monastery is part of the Kathina celebrations.*

Every year, Theravada Buddhist monks and nuns have a **retreat** during the rainy months. This was begun by the Buddha himself. They stay in the **monastery** and concentrate on their beliefs. Kathina takes place at the end of this time, November in the Western calendar. People take a gift of a robe to the monastery. This is to say 'thank you' to the monks for the work they do during the year, and it also shows that the people realize how important the monks are.

The cloth is usually given to the monastery so that the monks can cut it out and stitch it together in the proper way. The head of the monastery chooses one monk to receive the robe. In Thailand, it is traditional for the royal family to visit monasteries and give robes.

No monk owns things himself, so gifts are always given to the monastery. Giving at this time is thought to earn more **merit** for the giver.

The Buddha's teaching about how to live

If a man speaks many holy words but he speaks and does not, this thoughtless man cannot enjoy the life of holiness: he is like a cowherd who counts the cows of his master. Whereas if a man speaks but a few holy words, and yet he lives the life of those words, free from passion and hate and illusion … the life of this man in a life of holiness.

(Dhammapada 1:19–20)

Songkran

In Thailand, the festival of Songkran takes place in April and lasts for three days. It is the Thai New Year. The day before the festival begins, there is a procession of elephants through towns and villages. Houses and temples are cleaned and dusted, and rubbish is removed. This is all part of a fresh beginning for the festival. Everyone eats special foods, and wears new clothes. During the festival, Buddhists go to the monastery to give presents to the monks. These are things such as flowers, food and candles. This is another symbol that the new year is a chance to make a fresh start.

▲ *Spraying water at the processions is part of the fun of Songkran!*

Celebrating Songkran

Water is important in the celebrations of Songkran. Some people say that this recalls a story about the Buddha. The story says that once the king of a country through which the Buddha was travelling wanted to keep something to remember him by. The Buddha pressed his foot into the sand at the side of a river, and left the king his footprint. Boat races are held on rivers, and there are often water fights in the streets. The festival occurs during the dry season, when it is so hot that smaller rivers dry up. Fish are often trapped in ponds which form as the water evaporates. These fish are rescued by the people and kept until Songkran, when they are released into the deep river. Sometimes caged birds are set free, too. These customs follow the Buddha's teaching about how important it is to be kind to all living things. Buddhists believe that by setting the creatures free, they will gain merit.

Like all festivals, the celebrations take many different forms in different places. There is dancing and fireworks, and traditional shadow-plays. These use a screen with a light behind it, with puppets held so that their shadows fall on the screen. The puppets are attached to sticks, with strings so that their arms, legs and mouths can move. The figures act out traditional stories, with the puppeteers doing the talking. At midnight on the third day of the festival, monks in the monasteries strike a bell and beat a huge drum. The sound builds and dies away three times. After the third time, the festival is over for another year.

Celebrations – Poson and Esala Perahera

The festivals of Poson and Esala **Perahera** are held in Sri Lanka.

Poson

Poson is the name of the month which falls in June/July in the Western calendar. The festival – also called Poson – is held on the day of the full moon. It celebrates the time when Buddhism was first brought to Sri Lanka in 250 BCE. Buddhists believe that in that year the king of Sri Lanka asked Emperor Asoka to send a **missionary** so that he could hear for himself the teachings of the Buddha. The Emperor sent his son, a Buddhist **monk** called the **Venerable** Mahinda. He preached to the king, who immediately became a Buddhist. The king then asked the Emperor to send an Order of Buddhist **nuns** and the Emperor sent his daughter, the Venerable Sanghamitta. She arrived with a branch of the **bodhi tree** in a golden vase. This was planted and it grew. The tree still survives, in the city of Anaradhapura, near the town of Mihintale. The **monastery** there is called the Shri Maha Bodhi, and is named after the tree.

You can find the places mentioned in this book on the map on page 44.

Each year, there are processions called **peraheras**, with huge floats. They carry statues that tell the story of Mahinda coming to Sri Lanka. The floats are surrounded by elephants wearing beautifully embroidered coats. Drummers follow the processions, and there are fireworks and dancing. The largest and most impressive processions are at Mihintale, the nearest town to where Mahinda first met the king.

◀ The monastery at Shri Maha Bodhi is named after the tree (in the background in this photo) which grew from the branch brought by the Venerable Sanghamitta in 250 CE.

Esala Perahera

Esala Day is the day on which Buddhists all over the world celebrate the Buddha's first sermon. In Sri Lanka, Esala Day is a national holiday. One of the most impressive celebrations is held in the town of Kandy, in central Sri Lanka. A Buddhist temple there was specially built to keep a **relic** of the Buddha – one of his teeth. This is kept locked away in a special **casket**. For fifteen days every August the festival of Esala Perahera is held in its honour. The most important part of the festival is the perahera, a procession lit by torches, which takes place on the night of the full moon. Over 100 elephants take part in the procession. They are beautifully decorated, and wear brightly coloured cloths. The leading elephant carries a casket which is an exact copy of the one which holds the Buddha's tooth. (The real one is far too important to be taken out of the temple.) Other elephants carry caskets with relics of other important Buddhists. The procession travels through the town, watched by huge crowds.

Esala Perahera is a religious festival, but it is also a time for enjoying yourself, and there is a carnival on the streets. Dancers, drummers and fire-eaters accompany the procession, and people light fireworks and burn **incense** and other sweet-smelling perfumes.

Elephants and Buddhist festivals

Many Buddhist festivals use elephants as part of the celebrations. There are obvious reasons for this – Buddhism is at its strongest in countries where elephants have been used for centuries as beasts of burden and for transport. However, Buddhists also say that it is appropriate that they take part in festival processions because the Buddha once used the example of an elephant in his teaching. He pointed out that when a wild elephant is caught, it does not know how to behave and cannot be any use to its new master. In those days, in order to teach it what to do, elephant trainers would harness a wild elephant to a trusted tame one. The idea was that the tame one could teach the wild one. The Buddha advised his followers that they should do something similar in order to learn about Buddhism – they should find a Buddhist whom they trusted, and learn from him or her. Watching elephants in the festivals reminds Buddhists of this teaching.

▲ *These elephants are being prepared for a perahera.*

Celebrations – some Mahayana Buddhist festivals

Mahayana Buddhists celebrate many of the same festivals as **Theravada** Buddhists, but in different ways.

Losar, a Tibetan Buddhist festival

Losar is the New Year festival for **Tibetan** Buddhists, and their most important festival of the year. It begins at the full moon in February, and lasts for fifteen days. During this time they remember the Buddha's early life, and the difficulties he had when he first began preaching. Like many other New Year celebrations in different countries, there is a lot of emphasis on a fresh start. As a sign of this, people clean and tidy homes and temples. There are torchlit processions led by **monks** wearing fancy dress. They wear frightening masks and perform special dances to scare away evil spirits.

The last and most important day of the festival is called Changa Chopa. There are plays about the Buddha's life, and monks hold puppet shows. The most spectacular part of the celebration involves sculptures of scenes from the Buddha's life. The

▲ *Sculptures made from butter are a traditional part of the celebrations at Changa Chopa, the last day of Losar.*

amazing thing is that the sculptures are made out of butter. They are carved into very intricate patterns, and coloured with special dyes. There are competitions and prizes are awarded for the best sculptures.

What the Buddha said about wisdom

This is the sort of teaching of the Buddha that Buddhists think about when they are planning their fresh starts at New Year.

If during the whole of his life a fool lives with a wise man, he never knows the path of wisdom, as the spoon never knows the taste of the soup.
But if a man who watches and sees is only a moment with a wise man, he knows the path of wisdom as the tongue knows the taste of the soup.

(Dhammapada 5:64-5)

Japanese New Year

The Japanese use the same calendar as people in Western countries, so New Year is 1 January. For Japanese Buddhists, New Year's Eve is more important. This is when the 'Evening Bells' ceremony takes place. At midnight, the bells in every Buddhist temple are struck 108 times. This is a special number for Buddhists, because many of them believe that it is the number of 'mortal passions'. These include feelings of envy, pride and jealousy which spoil people's lives and prevent them becoming good Buddhists. As the bells ring, Buddhists think about what has been wrong with their lives in the past year, and how they can improve them in the new year.

Obon, a Japanese festival

Obon takes place for four days in July. It is a family festival and, if possible, people go home to their parents to celebrate it. **Mahayana** Buddhists believe that the Buddha can help you in your life, and they pray to him during Obon. They also ask his help for relatives who have died. People visit the

▲ *This family is taking part in prayers at a shrine in Japan on New Year's Eve.*

graves of relatives. In some areas, spirits of dead relatives are thought to return to the family home, so lamps are lit to show them the way. In other places, there are bonfires. Obon is a serious festival, but it is also celebrated with fairs and dancing. A dance where everyone joins hands and dances round in a circle gives the festival its name.

Higan, a Japanese festival

Higan takes place at the times of the equinoxes. These are the two times in the year when day and night are of equal length. It is also the time when the seasons begin to change. This reminds Buddhists that they need to change their lives so they can reach **Enlightenment**. Higan is a time for remembering friends and relatives who have died. Buddhists go to cemeteries to clean and look after the graves, and decorate them with flowers. This reminds them that, like flowers, nothing in life is permanent and their relatives have gone on to a better life. There are special ceremonies which they believe give **merit** to people who have died. This is important, because they believe the extra merit can help the dead on their way to **Nirvana**.

Family occasions – young people

Buddhists believe there is no such thing as a soul which lives on after death. Buddhism teaches that the way you live is what is important, and birth and death are just stages on the way to the next life. Therefore, there are very few teachings in Buddhism about the beginning and ending of life. However, for most people, the arrival of a new baby or the death of someone they love is a very important event. Most Buddhists follow the customs of their country. This means that Buddhists in different countries may have quite different customs, because the celebrations are connected to the culture rather than to Buddhism.

In **Theravada** Buddhist countries, the main ceremonies for a baby happen when he or she is a month old. Its head is shaved, because the hair is a symbol of a bad **kamma** (life-force) from a previous life. Coloured threads which have been blessed are tied around the baby's wrists. **Monks** are often invited to this ceremony and may be asked to suggest a name for the baby. They prepare a horoscope based on the exact moment of birth. The family always give food to the monks when a baby is born.

Joining a monastery

Many Buddhist boys join a **monastery** for at least a few months. This often happens when they are in their teens or their early twenties, but in Myanmar and Thailand almost all boys join when they are ten or even younger. A boy who joins the monastery at this age is not expected to stay there all his life. Many boys stay for a few years so that they can be educated by the monks.

▼ *Boys at a ceremony for becoming Zen Buddhist monks.*

Celebrations in Myanmar

In Myanmar, the ceremony when a boy becomes a monk is called the **Pravrajya ceremony**. The boy acts out the story of how Siddattha left his comfortable palace and became a wandering monk. He is dressed like a prince and leads a procession though the streets of his home town, riding a donkey or pony. When they reach the monastery, he asks the monks if he may be allowed to enter. First, he takes off his prince's clothes, and older monks help him put on the plain orange robe of a Theravada monk. His head and his eyebrows are shaved. Most Buddhist monks have shaved heads, to show that they do not care about their appearance. The boy promises to obey the Ten **Precepts** which all Buddhist monks follow, and he is given a new name. This is always from the ancient **Pali** language, and he uses it for as long as he is a monk. Sometimes, a boy's parents give him other presents – a spare robe, or the bowl in which he will collect his food.

▲ *An older monk shaves the boy's head as part of the preparations for becoming a monk.*

If a Buddhist girl becomes a **nun**, she goes through the same ceremony as a boy. However, most girls do not become nuns. In Myanmar, there is a special ceremony for Buddhist girls, which occurs on the day that her brother has his Pravrajya ceremony. The girl is dressed in expensive clothes and has her earlobes pierced with a golden needle. This is believed to be a symbol to show that one day she will marry and wear the fine jewellery that it is traditional for women in Myanmar to wear on their wedding day.

Duties to a son

The **Buddha** said that parents have duties to their son which they must perform. These are to keep him from harm, to show him the right way to live, to teach him, to choose a good wife for him, and to make sure that he has something to inherit. In return, a son is expected to respect his parents and look after them when necessary. He should respect the dead, and keep up the honour of his family.

Family occasions – marriage and death

Marriage

Like other family ceremonies, Buddhist marriages may be quite different in different countries, because they mainly reflect the country and the culture in which the couple live. In most Buddhist countries, marriages have traditionally been 'arranged' – a young person's parents or older relatives make enquiries about someone who may be a suitable partner. Today, it is becoming more common for a young person to suggest someone they know, and the couple usually meet a few times before the wedding. Both have the right to refuse but, if they agree to the marriage, astrologers (people who tell the future from the stars) are usually asked to suggest a good date for the wedding to take place.

In Buddhist countries, a wedding usually takes place in the bride's home. The ceremony is usually performed by a male relative of the bride, rather than a **monk**. The couple stand on a special platform called a purowa, which is decorated with white flowers. They usually exchange rings, and the thumbs of their right hands are tied together. Sometimes their right wrists are tied with a silk scarf, instead. This is a symbol that they are being joined as husband and wife. Children recite particular parts of the Buddhist holy books, and the couple repeat promises that they will respect and be faithful to each other.

As part of the wedding, a monk may give a talk about the Buddha's teaching on marriage. If this does not happen, the couple usually go to the **monastery** together, before or after the wedding, and listen to the Buddha's teaching there. At the end of the ceremony, everyone shares a meal. The celebrations may go on for several days.

◀ *A traditional Buddhist wedding procession taking place in Hong Kong.*

Death

Like other family events, Buddhist funerals reflect the customs of the country in which the person lived. They concentrate on reflecting the person's life, and how they touched other people's lives. The Buddha's teaching emphasized how everything is connected and nothing lasts. A monk may give a talk about the Buddha's teaching, and everyone repeats the Five **Precepts** and the Three Jewels. In some countries, it is usual for a dead body to be **cremated**, and the ashes may be collected and placed in a stupa. In other countries, burial is more common. In **Tibetan** Buddhism, only the body of the **Dalai Lama** is cremated.

When someone dies, their relatives often give gifts to the monks. A common gift is the material for a new robe. They ask that the **merit** they gain from doing this should be shared with the person who has died. They believe that this may help the person. For the same reason, Buddhists always look after graves very carefully. At festivals every year, there are ceremonies to 'pass on' merit to the person who has died. Buddhists believe that consciousness exists for three days after death, so there are readings from the holy books during this time.

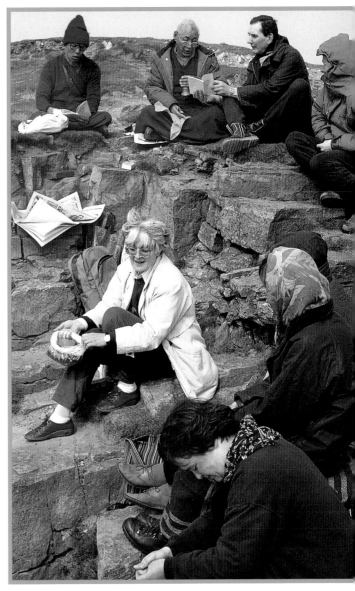

▲ These Buddhists are taking part in a ceremony on a Welsh mountain top (UK), to mark the death of a Buddhist **nun**, and to scatter her ashes.

MinHan's view

MinHan is 16 and comes from Malaysia.

My grandfather died last year. It was the first time anyone close to me has died. I found the funeral very moving. It was very dignified and solemn, but it was as if everyone there remembered that death really is just a stepping stone to another life. My father and my uncle, his sons, spoke about Grandfather's life and the sort of person he was – my uncle told a couple of stories about him that made us laugh. Then a monk we know spoke about the Buddha's teaching. At the end I still felt sad, and it was strange to know that I will never talk to him again, but I felt sure that everything was right. He had lived a good life, and that was important.

What it means to be a Buddhist

As individuals

Buddhists try to follow the teachings of the Buddha by following the Eightfold Path, or Middle Way. This tries to avoid extremes, so Buddhists do not choose to live in luxury or in extreme poverty. All Buddhists try to keep the Five **Precepts**, so they try to live in a way that does not harm any other living being. For example, many Buddhists avoid jobs such as manufacturing guns or weapons, or selling tobacco or alcohol.

How Buddhists live depends on which country in the world they live in. However, Buddhism teaches high standards of behaviour, and many Buddhists are pacifists, who believe that it is wrong to fight. There are strong traditions of hospitality, and Buddhism teaches that strangers are to be treated with respect and kindness.

▲ *Giving food to a monk in Japan.*

The Buddha said that family life was important. According to Buddhist teaching, husbands should look after and care for their wives, and treat them with consideration and respect. In return, a wife should look after her husband and care for the home and children. Children are expected to respect their parents, which includes previous generations who have died.

Going for Refuge

Buddhists do not actively try to persuade people to become Buddhists but, especially in recent years, many people in Western countries have become interested in Buddhism. They see in it a system of thinking which does not ask them to accept anything that they have not worked out for themselves, and many people feel that they can identify with its teaching about caring for others and the world. The ceremony in which someone becomes a Buddhist is very simple. It is called 'Going for Refuge'. The person states in front of witnesses that they wish to take the Buddha as their guide, that they will follow his teachings, and that they wish to become part of the Buddhist community.

In the community

In the days of the Buddha, the **Sangha** meant the entire Buddhist community. Today, Sangha usually refers only to Buddhist **monks** and **nuns**. **Mahayana** Buddhists often use the word to mean a community of followers. Buddhists have a strong sense of community with other Buddhists, no matter where in the world they live. They often refer to other Buddhists as 'spiritual friends'. The Buddha told his followers to join together and help each other, and that this would help them to become more like him.

Buddhism does not have set days for worship, but many ordinary Buddhists go to the **monastery** or temple on the days of the new moon and the full moon. These days are called Uposatha days. The people take food and other gifts to the monks, and join in their **meditation**. Buddhism teaches that giving gifts to the monks will earn **merit** for the giver. The idea of giving to others (dana) is very important in Buddhism. The Buddha taught that the more you give, the less selfish you will become. Buddhist monks do not beg, because it is understood that the gifts they receive are in return for the teaching which is given to the people.

In the world

In the last 20 or 30 years, the ideas that Buddhism has been teaching for centuries have become much more widely accepted. Concern for the environment, and for treating the world as a resource to be cared for, are at the heart of Buddhism. The concern for all living things means that involvement with non-violent pressure groups is in agreement with Buddhist teaching.

▶ *An organic farming site in Ladakh in the Himalayas, an example of Buddhists caring for the environment.*

The message of Buddhism

This is a saying which is often repeated at Buddhist festivals, and which is one way of summing up what Buddhists try to achieve in their lives.

Close your eyes and you will see clearly,
Cease to listen and you will hear the truth,
Be silent, and your heart will sing,
Be gentle and you will need no strength,
Be patient and you will achieve all things.

Map

The globe on the right shows the location of the map below.

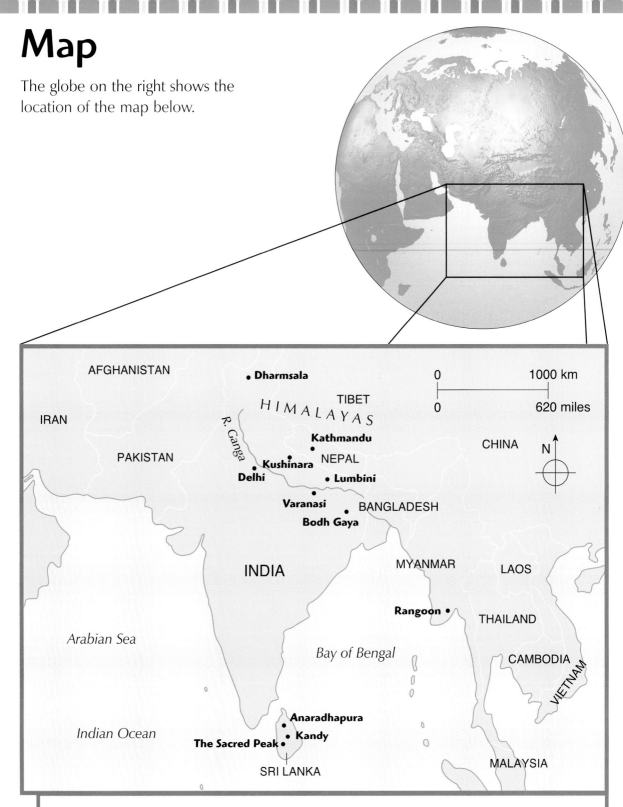

Place names

Some places on this map, or mentioned in the book, have been known by different names:

Kushinara – Kushinagara   Sri Lanka – Ceylon

Myanmar – Burma   Varanasi – Benares.

River Ganga – River Ganges

Timechart

Major events in world history

BCE	3000–1700	Indus valley civilization flourished
	2500	Pyramids in Egypt built
	1800	Stonehenge completed
	1220	Rameses II builds the Temple of Amon (Egypt)
	1000	Nubian Empire (countries around the Nile) begins & lasts until c350CE
	776	First Olympic games
	450s	Greece is a centre of art and literature under Pericles
	336–323	Conquests of Alexander the Great
	300	Mayan civilization begins
	200	Great Wall of China begun
	48	Julius Caesar becomes Roman emperor
CE	79	Eruption of Vesuvius destroys Pompeii
	161–80	Golden Age of the Roman Empire under Marcus Aurelius
	330	Byzantine Empire begins
	868	First printed book (China)
	c1000	Leif Ericson may have discovered America
	1066	Battle of Hastings, Norman Conquest of Britain
	1300	Ottoman empire begins (lasts until 1922)
	1325	Aztec Empire begins (lasts until 1521)
	1400	Black Death kills one person in three throughout China, North Africa and Europe
	1452	Leonardo da Vinci born
	1492	Christopher Columbus sails to America
	1564	William Shakespeare born
	1620	Pilgrim Fathers arrive in what is now Massachusetts
	1648	Taj Mahal built
	1768–71	Captain Cook sails to Australia
	1776	American Declaration of Independence
	1859	Charles Darwin publishes *Origin of Species*
	1908	Henry Ford produces the first Model T Ford car
	1914–18	World War I
	1929	Wall Street Crash and the Great Depression
	1939–45	World War II
	1946	First computer invented
	1953	Chemical structure of DNA discovered
	1969	First moon landings
	1981	AIDS virus diagnosed
	1984	Scientists discover a hole in the ozone layer
	1989	Berlin Wall is torn down
	1991	Break-up of the former Soviet Union
	1994	Nelson Mandela becomes President of South Africa
	1997	An adult mammal, Dolly the Sheep, is cloned for the first time
	2000	Millennium celebrations take place all over the world.

Major events in Buddhist history

BCE	c563	Gotama Buddha born
	c528	Buddha achieves Enlightenment
	c483	Buddha passes away
	273–232	Emperor Asoka of India
	c200	Beginnings of Mahayana Buddhism (Madhyamika school)
	c100	Holy books written down for the first time
CE	c100	Buddhism becomes established in Tibet and Nepal
	c150	First Buddhist monastery established in China
	c400	Huiyuan (founder of Pure Land school)
	c500	Buddhism becomes established in Korea
	c700	Zhiyi (monk who founded the Tendai school, Japan)
	868	Diamond Sutra printed in China (first ever printed book)
	c1100	King Anawratha (Burma)
	1222–1282	Nichiren school begun
	c1800	Buddhism spreads to the west coast of America
	1893	First Buddhist missionary arrives in UK
	1959	Chinese invade Tibet – Dalai Lama flees to India.

Glossary

alms	giving food and necessities
anatta	Buddhist belief that there is 'no-soul'
anicca	Buddhist belief in impermanence, that nothing lasts
bhikkhu	Buddhist monk
bhikkhuni	Buddhist nun
bodhi tree	tree under which the Buddha was sitting when he gained Enlightenment
Bodhisattva	someone who has chosen to be reborn after gaining Enlightenment, so that they can help others to achieve it
Buddha	one who has gained Enlightenment (Siddattha Gotama)
Buddharupa	image of the Buddha
canon	approved collection of teaching
casket	decorated container
cremate	burn a body after death
Dalai Lama	leader of Tibetan Buddhists
dana	generosity, giving to others
dhamma (or dharma)	the Buddha's teaching
Diamond Sutra	important Mahayana Buddhist teaching
dukkha	Buddhist belief that everything in the world is 'unsatisfactory'
Enlightenment	understanding the truth about the way things are
fast	go without food or drink for religious reasons
incense	spice which burns with a strong sweet smell
kamma (or karma)	life-force which a person creates during life
lotus position	position for meditation in which the person sits cross-legged, with the sole of each foot resting on the opposite thigh.
Lotus sutra	important Mahayana Buddhist teaching
Mahayana	'greater vehicle' school of Buddhism
mandala	specially designed pattern made up of circles, squares and triangles.
mantra	word or phrase repeated as a prayer and as an aid to meditation
meditation	mental control which leads to concentration and calmness
merit	reward for doing good things
missionary	someone who travels to tell people about his or her beliefs

monastery	place where monks live
monk	man who has dedicated his life to religion
mudras	symbolic hand gestures
Nirvana (Nibbana)	the end of imperfection
nun	woman who has dedicated her life to religion
Pali	ancient language
Parinirvana (Parinibbana)	the final passing away of a Buddha
perahera	procession which is part of a festival
philosophy	a system of thinking
pilgrimage	journey made for religious reasons
Pravrajya ceremony	ceremony in which a boy becomes a monk
precept	guide for living
Pure Land	school of Mahayana Buddhism
rebirth	Buddhist belief that the five parts of a person re-form to make a new person
reincarnation	belief that after death a soul is reborn
relic	something which is old and treasured (often the remains of a holy person)
retreat	special time for meditation (usually in a monastery)
rupa	statue (of the Buddha)
samsara	the cycle of birth, death and 'rebecoming' which Buddhists believe in
Sangha	community (today, used to describe Buddhist monks and nuns)
Sanskrit	ancient Indian language
shrine	special place of worship
stupa	burial mound erected to house the ashes of the Buddha or another important Buddhist
Sukhavati	the Pure Land (paradise) in Pure Land Buddhist teaching
sutta (sutra)	small piece of teaching
Theravada	'teachings of the elders' – a school of Buddhism
Tibetan	from Tibet – a school of Buddhism
Tipitaka	'three baskets' – the most important Buddhist teachings
vajra	symbolic thunderbolt, representing the way Enlightenment comes like a bolt of lightning
Venerable	very respected – a title for Buddhist monks
vihara	Buddhist monastery
Zen	'meditation' – a school of Buddhism

Index

Titles in the *World Beliefs And Cultures* series include:

Hardback   0 431 09311 3

Hardback   0 431 09310 5

Hardback   0 431 09312 1

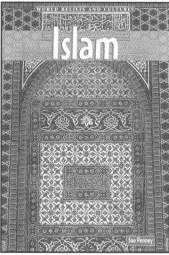

Hardback   0 431 09313 X

Hardback   0 431 09314 8

Hardback   0 431 09315 6

Find out about the other titles in this series on our website www.heinemann.co.uk/library